Pasta for the Senses

S.R. Moore

Published by S.R. Moore, 2023.

PASTA FOR THE SENSES

First edition. December 26, 2023.

ISBN: 979-8224242856

Written by S.R. Moore.

Also by S.R. Moore

Mysteries of Lavender Lane
The Secret of Lavender Lane
The Book Club Conspiracy
The Mosaic Murders

Standalone
Pizza Artistry: The Canvas of Flavor
Brews & Bites: A Beer Cheese Revolution
Souper Fusion: A Globetrotter's Culinary Journey in a Bowl
Slices of Heaven: Sandwiches Redefined for the Modern Foodie
Advent Cookies Around the World: A Global Gastronomic Journey
Pasta for the Senses
Shamrock & Spoon: Modern Irish Cooking for Every Occasion

Table of Contents

Introduction

Welcome to "Pasta for the Senses," a cookbook that is not just a collection of recipes but an invitation to experience the art of cooking and dining in a wholly immersive way. Born out of a deep love for pasta and a fascination with the sensory richness of cooking, this book aims to transform your kitchen into a stage for sensory exploration.

Pasta, in its myriad forms, is more than just comfort food; it is a canvas for culinary creativity. Each chapter in this cookbook is a celebration of one of the five senses: sight, smell, taste, touch, and sound. The recipes have been meticulously crafted not only for their flavors but also for their ability to engage and delight your senses.

Imagine the vibrant colors of a Rainbow Vegetable Tagliatelle, the sizzle and aroma of garlic and bacon in a skillet, the comforting warmth of freshly baked Mac and Cheese, the tender bite of al dente Spaghetti, and the visually stunning twirl of Fettuccine. "Pasta for the Senses" guides you through these experiences, making every meal an occasion to savor in more ways than one.

Whether you are an experienced cook or just beginning your culinary journey, this book is designed to inspire you. Beyond the recipes, you'll find stories, tips, and ideas that encourage you to experiment and personalize your cooking. The sensory-focused approach offers a new way to think about and appreciate the simple act of making a meal.

As you turn these pages, I invite you to join me in celebrating the symphony of senses that pasta cooking and eating can be. Let's create dishes that not only nourish the body but also feed the soul and awaken every sense. Welcome to a world where every forkful is an exploration, and every meal, a delightful discovery.

Your journey through the senses awaits. Let's begin.

Cooking Tips and Techniques

Welcome to the exciting world of pasta cooking! Whether you're a beginner or a seasoned home chef, these tips and techniques will enhance your culinary skills and elevate your pasta dishes.

Cooking Methods

1. **Perfect Pasta**: For al dente pasta, cook it in abundant salted boiling water. Check it a couple of minutes before the package instructions suggest; it should be tender but firm to the bite.

2. **Sauce Simmering**: Allow your sauces to simmer gently. This slow cooking process melds the flavors together and enhances the depth of the sauce.

3. **Roasting Vegetables**: To roast vegetables evenly, cut them into uniform sizes and toss with oil, salt, and pepper. Roast in a preheated oven until tender and slightly caramelized.

Ingredient Substitutions

1. **Cheese Alternatives**: If you're out of Parmesan, try Grana Padano or Pecorino Romano for a similar salty and umami flavor.

2. **Pasta Varieties**: Don't have the specific pasta type a recipe calls for? Most shapes can be substituted for one another based on what you have – the key is to match the sauce's consistency with the pasta's shape.

3. **Herb Replacements**: Fresh herbs bring a dish to life. If you don't have fresh basil, try fresh parsley or even a touch of dried herbs in a pinch.

Kitchen Tools

1. **Pasta Pot**: Invest in a large pasta pot with plenty of room for water, allowing the pasta to cook evenly without sticking.

2. **Strainer or Colander**: Essential for draining pasta. A strainer with fine mesh is great for catching small pasta shapes.
3. **Skillet or Sauté Pan**: A large skillet is ideal for sautéing vegetables and simmering sauces.

Presentation Skills

1. **Garnishing**: Add fresh herbs or a sprinkle of cheese just before serving to enhance the appearance and flavor of the dish.
2. **Plating**: Use a white plate for a clean, elegant presentation that makes the colors of the pasta and sauce pop.
3. **Portion Size**: Serve moderate portions to make the dish look ample and appetizing without overwhelming the plate.

Remember, cooking is an art and a science. Feel free to experiment and adjust recipes to suit your taste and sensory preferences. Most importantly, have fun and enjoy the process of creating delightful pasta dishes!

Ingredient Guide

Understanding and using the right ingredients can elevate your pasta dishes to new heights. Here's a guide to some less common ingredients you'll encounter in this cookbook, their flavors, how to select and store them, and possible substitutes.

1. Mascarpone Cheese
Flavor: Creamy, mild, and slightly sweet.
Selection & Storage: Choose fresh mascarpone with a smooth texture. Store in the refrigerator and use within a few days of opening.
Substitute: A mix of cream cheese and heavy cream can mimic its texture and taste.

2. Kalamata Olives
Flavor: Bold, briny, and a bit smoky.
Selection & Storage: Look for olives that are plump and glossy. Store in a brine solution in the refrigerator.
Substitute: Black olives, though less robust, can be an alternative.

3. Pine Nuts
Flavor: Buttery, creamy, and slightly sweet when toasted.
Selection & Storage: Choose plump, unblemished nuts. Store in an airtight container in the fridge or freezer as they can go rancid quickly.
Substitute: Slivered almonds or chopped walnuts, though less buttery, can provide a similar crunch.

4. Arborio Rice
Flavor: Starchy and creamy when cooked, ideal for risotto.
Selection & Storage: Look for short, plump grains. Store in a cool, dry place.

Substitute: Carnaroli or Vialone Nano rice, or in a pinch, regular short-grain rice.

5. Capers

Flavor: Tangy, lemony, and salty.

Selection & Storage: Often found in brine, choose capers that are firm. Store in the refrigerator after opening.

Substitute: Chopped green olives can mimic their brininess.

6. Truffle Oil

Flavor: Earthy, musky, and pungent.

Selection & Storage: Look for high-quality oil with real truffle essence. Store in a cool, dark place.

Substitute: Porcini mushroom powder or a tiny bit of mushroom stock can give an earthy flavor.

7. Anchovy Paste

Flavor: Salty, fishy, and umami-rich.

Selection & Storage: Available in tubes for easy use. Store in the refrigerator after opening.

Substitute: Soy sauce or Worcestershire sauce can provide a similar depth of flavor.

8. Saffron

Flavor: Slightly sweet, floral, and earthy.

Selection & Storage: Look for bright red threads without any yellow parts. Store in a cool, dark place.

Substitute: Turmeric can mimic its color, though not its distinct flavor.

9. Pecorino Romano Cheese

Flavor: Sharp, salty, and tangy.

Selection & Storage: Opt for a wedge and grate as needed. Store wrapped in parchment paper in the refrigerator.

Substitute: Parmesan, while less sharp, can be used for a similar texture.

Understanding these ingredients and how to effectively use and substitute them can make a significant difference in your cooking. Always remember, the key to great cuisine is the quality of ingredients you use.

Meal Planning and Pairing Suggestions

Creating a well-rounded meal is about more than just the main dish. It's about complementing flavors, textures, and creating a satisfying dining experience. Here are some meal planning and pairing suggestions to help you make the most of the recipes in "Pasta for the Senses."

Meal Planning Ideas

1. Italian Night
- **Main:** Classic Spaghetti Marinara
- **Side:** Garlic Bread or a Simple Green Salad with Balsamic Vinaigrette
- **Dessert:** Tiramisu or Gelato
- **Drink:** Chianti or a refreshing Aperol Spritz

2. Mediterranean Feast
- **Main:** Greek Pasta Salad
- **Side:** Hummus with Pita Bread
- **Dessert:** Baklava or Greek Yogurt with Honey
- **Drink:** Retsina or a glass of Ouzo

3. Cozy Comfort Food
- **Main:** Baked Mac and Cheese
- **Side:** Steamed Broccoli or a Caesar Salad
- **Dessert:** Warm Apple Pie or Chocolate Brownies
- **Drink:** Apple Cider or a Rich Cabernet Sauvignon

4. Summer Pasta Party
- **Main:** Popping Cherry Tomato and Basil Penne
- **Side:** Grilled Vegetable Skewers or Caprese Salad
- **Dessert:** Lemon Sorbet or Fruit Salad
- **Drink:** White Sangria or Sparkling Lemonade

5. Asian-Inspired Evening
- **Main:** Slippery Egg Noodles with Sesame Sauce
- **Side:** Asian Slaw or Dumplings
- **Dessert:** Mango Sticky Rice or Matcha Ice Cream
- **Drink:** Sake or Jasmine Tea

Tips for Successful Pairings

1. Balance Flavors: If your main dish is rich and heavy, pair it with a light, refreshing side or drink.

2. Complement Textures: A creamy pasta might pair well with a crisp salad or crusty bread.

3. Consider Themes: Stick to a regional theme for a cohesive culinary experience.

4. Dessert Pairings: Choose desserts that complement or contrast the main meal's flavors.

5. Beverage Choices: Select beverages that enhance the meal – wine for sophistication, cocktails for fun, or tea/coffee for a comforting touch.

By considering these pairing suggestions, you can create memorable meals that tantalize all the senses. Remember, the best pairings are those that suit your taste and bring joy to your dining experience.

"Pasta for the Senses" is designed to cater to a variety of dining experiences, moods, and occasions. The recipes are organized into thematic sections, making it easy for you to find the perfect dish for any moment.

1. Sensory Feasts
- Focused on recipes that engage all senses, like Rainbow Vegetable Tagliatelle or Sizzling Bacon and Tomato Spaghetti.
- Ideal for: Those who love a full sensory experience in their meals.

2. Quick and Easy
- Features recipes that can be whipped up in no time, like Garlic and Olive Oil Spaghetti (Aglio e Olio) or Crunchy Walnut and Spinach Pesto Farfalle.
- Ideal for: Busy weeknights or when you need a quick yet delicious meal.

3. Comfort Classics
- Homey, comforting dishes such as Baked Mac and Cheese or Creamy Gorgonzola and Walnut Fettuccine.
- Ideal for: Cozy nights in, comfort food cravings, or family dinners.

4. Light and Fresh
- Includes lighter pasta options like Lemon and Asparagus Spaghetti or Caprese Pasta Salad.
- Ideal for: Summer days, health-conscious meals, or a light lunch.

5. Festive and Fancy

- Special occasion recipes that are sure to impress, such as Truffle and Mushroom Tagliatelle or Saffron Linguine with Clams.
- Ideal for: Celebrations, date nights, or when you want to indulge.

6. Global Inspirations
- A collection of pasta dishes inspired by flavors from around the world, like Umami Mushroom Ravioli in Soy Butter Sauce or Slippery Egg Noodles with Sesame Sauce.
- Ideal for: Adventurous eaters or themed dinner nights.

7. Seasonal Sensations
- Season-specific recipes, perfect for using fresh, seasonal ingredients, such as Pumpkin and Ricotta Stuffed Ravioli in fall or Zucchini Ribbon Pappardelle with Pesto in summer.
- Ideal for: Seasonal cooking and making the most of fresh produce.

8. Dessert Pastas
- Unique pasta-based desserts like Cinnamon and Pumpkin Lasagna or Sweet and Sour Sicilian Caponata Pasta.
- Ideal for: Dessert lovers and those looking to try something new.

Each section offers a unique culinary journey, inviting you to explore the vast and versatile world of pasta. Whether you're in the mood for something quick and easy or a dish to dazzle your guests, "Pasta for the Senses" has you covered.

1. Rainbow Vegetable Tagliatelle: A vibrant medley of colorful vegetables intertwined with tagliatelle.

2. Black Ink Spaghetti with Seafood: Striking black pasta with a colorful assortment of seafood.

3. Beetroot Gnocchi with Sage Butter: Vivid pink gnocchi, contrasting beautifully with the green sage.

4. Saffron Linguine with Clams: Golden-hued pasta with a shimmering, creamy sauce.

5. Pumpkin and Ricotta Stuffed Ravioli: Bright orange pumpkin filling peeking through delicate pasta.

6. Tri-Color Rotini Salad: Spirals of green, white, and red, adorned with vibrant veggies.

7. Zucchini Ribbon Pappardelle with Pesto: Green and yellow zucchini ribbons in a lush pesto sauce.

8. Butterfly Pea Flower Fettuccine with Alfredo: Naturally blue pasta with a classic white Alfredo sauce.

Rainbow Vegetable Tagliatelle

Ingredients:
- 300g tagliatelle pasta
- 1 red bell pepper, thinly sliced
- 2 carrots, julienned
- 1 yellow squash, thinly sliced
- 1 green zucchini, thinly sliced
- 1/2 purple cabbage, shredded
- 3 cloves of garlic, minced
- 2 tbsp olive oil
- Salt and pepper, to taste
- Fresh herbs (basil or parsley), for garnish
- Grated Parmesan cheese (optional)

Instructions:

1. Preparation: Cook the tagliatelle according to package instructions until al dente. Drain and set aside. In a large skillet, heat olive oil over medium heat.

2. Cooking the Vegetables: Add garlic and sauté for 1 minute. Add the red bell pepper and carrots, and cook for about 2 minutes. Then add the squash, zucchini, and purple cabbage. Stir-fry the vegetables until they are tender but still crisp.

3. Combining: Toss the cooked tagliatelle with the vegetables in the skillet. Season with salt and pepper to taste.

4. Garnishing: Serve the pasta garnished with fresh herbs and, if desired, a sprinkle of Parmesan cheese.

PASTA FOR THE SENSES

The Story Behind the Dish

Imagine a painter's palette, but instead of paints, you have the vibrant hues of fresh vegetables. This dish was inspired by the natural beauty of a summer garden, where colors are as much a part of the meal as flavors. Each vegetable not only adds its unique color but also its distinct taste and texture, creating a harmonious blend that delights both the eyes and the palate.

Tips and Tricks

- **Vibrancy in Cooking:** To keep the vegetables vibrant, cook them briefly. The goal is to soften them slightly while retaining their bright colors and crisp texture.
- **Pasta Cooking:** For the best texture, cook the pasta until it's just al dente. It will continue to cook slightly when tossed with the warm vegetables.
- **Customization:** Feel free to add or substitute vegetables based on seasonality and preference. The key is to maintain a rainbow of colors.
- **Flavor Enhancement:** A splash of lemon juice or white wine can add a bright, acidic note that enhances the flavors of the vegetables.

Black Ink Spaghetti with Seafood

Ingredients:
- 300g black ink spaghetti
- 200g mixed seafood (shrimp, scallops, mussels, calamari)
- 2 cloves of garlic, minced
- 1/2 cup white wine
- 2 tbsp olive oil
- Juice of 1 lemon
- Fresh parsley, chopped
- Salt and pepper, to taste
- Lemon wedges, for serving

Instructions:
1. **Pasta Preparation:** Cook the black ink spaghetti in salted boiling water until al dente. Drain and set aside.
2. **Cooking the Seafood:** In a large skillet, heat the olive oil over medium heat. Add the garlic and sauté until fragrant. Add the mixed seafood and cook until they start to turn opaque.
3. **Deglazing and Simmering:** Pour in the white wine and lemon juice, and let it simmer for a few minutes until the alcohol cooks off.
4. **Combining:** Toss the cooked spaghetti with the seafood and sauce in the skillet. Season with salt and pepper to taste.
5. **Garnishing and Serving:** Serve the pasta garnished with chopped parsley and lemon wedges on the side.

The Story Behind the Dish
Black Ink Spaghetti with Seafood is a celebration of the sea's mysteries and treasures. The black ink, traditionally from cuttlefish or squid, represents the deep, dark depths of the ocean, while the assortment of seafood brings the vibrancy of marine life to your plate. This dish is a favorite in coastal regions, where the connection to the sea is a vital part of culinary culture.

Tips and Tricks
- **Quality of Ingredients:** The key to this dish is the quality of the seafood. Fresh, high-quality seafood makes all the difference.
- **Cooking Seafood:** Be careful not to overcook the seafood. Each type has its own cooking time – shrimp and scallops take less time compared to mussels and calamari.
- **Ink Pasta:** If you can't find black ink spaghetti, you can use regular spaghetti and add squid ink to the cooking water for a similar effect.
- **Wine Pairing:** A crisp white wine pairs beautifully with this dish, complementing the seafood flavors.

Beetroot Gnocchi with Sage Butter

Ingredients:
- 2 large beetroots
- 400g all-purpose flour
- 1 egg
- 100g butter
- Fresh sage leaves
- Grated Parmesan cheese, for serving

Instructions:
1. **Beetroot Preparation:** Roast the beetroots in the oven until tender, let them cool, peel, and then puree them.
2. **Making the Gnocchi Dough:** Mix the beetroot puree with flour, egg, and a pinch of salt to form a dough. If it's too sticky, add a bit more flour.
3. **Shaping the Gnocchi:** Roll the dough into long snakes, cut into small pieces, and press with a fork to create ridges.
4. **Cooking the Gnocchi:** Boil the gnocchi in salted water until they float to the surface, then drain.
5. **Preparing the Sage Butter:** In a pan, melt the butter over medium heat and add the sage leaves. Cook until the butter gets a golden color and the sage is crispy.
6. **Combining:** Toss the cooked gnocchi in the sage butter.
7. **Serving:** Serve the gnocchi garnished with crispy sage leaves and grated Parmesan cheese.

The Story Behind the Dish

Beetroot Gnocchi with Sage Butter is a dish that tells a story of contrast and harmony. The earthy sweetness of beetroot pairs beautifully with the rich, aromatic sage butter. Originating from the heart of Italian cuisine, where color and flavor go hand in hand, this dish brings a modern twist to traditional gnocchi.

Tips and Tricks

- **Consistency of Dough:** The key to perfect gnocchi is the dough consistency. It should be soft but not too sticky. Adjust with flour as needed.
- **Roasting Beetroots:** Roasting intensifies the sweet flavor of the beets, which complements the savory butter sauce.
- **Butter Quality:** Use good quality butter for the sage sauce as it's the flavor base of the dish.
- **Serving Suggestion:** For an extra flavor, sprinkle some crushed walnuts or pine nuts over the gnocchi before serving.

Saffron Linguine with Clams

Ingredients:
- 400g linguine
- 1g saffron threads
- 2 tbsp olive oil
- 4 cloves of garlic, minced
- 1/2 cup white wine
- 500g fresh clams, cleaned
- 1 cup heavy cream
- Fresh parsley, chopped
- Lemon zest, for garnish

Instructions:
1. Pasta Preparation: Cook the linguine in salted boiling water until al dente. Reserve some pasta water for later.

2. Saffron Infusion: Soak the saffron threads in a small amount of warm water to release their color and flavor.

3. Cooking the Clams: In a large skillet, heat olive oil over medium heat. Add garlic and sauté until fragrant. Add the clams and white wine, cover, and cook until the clams open. Remove the clams, leaving the liquid in the skillet.

4. Creating the Sauce: Add the saffron infusion and heavy cream to the skillet. Simmer until the sauce thickens slightly. Season with salt and pepper.

5. Combining: Add the cooked linguine to the sauce, tossing to coat. If the sauce is too thick, add some reserved pasta water.

6. Serving: Serve the pasta with the clams on top, garnished with chopped parsley and lemon zest.

The Story Behind the Dish

Saffron Linguine with Clams is a dish that speaks of coastal elegance. The use of saffron, a spice more precious than gold, adds a touch of luxury to the simple, briny flavor of clams. This dish is reminiscent of sun-kissed Mediterranean shores, where the finest ingredients are used to create flavors that are both rich and delicate.

Tips and Tricks

- **Quality of Saffron:** Use high-quality saffron for the best flavor and color. It's an investment that pays off in taste.
- **Freshness of Clams:** Ensure the clams are fresh and properly cleaned to avoid any grittiness in the dish.
- **Sauce Consistency:** The sauce should coat the linguine nicely but not be too thick. Adjust with pasta water as needed.
- **Wine Pairing:** Pair this dish with a light white wine that complements the delicate flavors of saffron and clams.

Pumpkin and Ricotta Stuffed Ravioli

Ingredients:
For the Ravioli:
- 200g all-purpose flour
- 2 large eggs
For the Filling:
- 1 cup pumpkin puree
- 1 cup ricotta cheese
- 1/4 cup grated Parmesan cheese
- Nutmeg, a pinch
For the Sauce:
- 100g butter
- Fresh sage leaves
- Roasted pumpkin seeds, for garnish

Instructions:
1. Making the Dough: Mix the flour, eggs, and salt to form a smooth pasta dough. Let it rest for 30 minutes.
2. Preparing the Filling: Combine pumpkin puree, ricotta, Parmesan, salt, pepper, and nutmeg.
3. Assembling the Ravioli: Roll out the dough thinly. Place small amounts of filling on the dough, cover with another layer of dough, and cut into ravioli shapes. Seal the edges well.
4. Cooking the Ravioli: Cook the ravioli in boiling salted water until they float to the surface. Drain them gently.
5. Making the Sauce: Melt the butter in a pan and add the sage leaves. Cook until the butter gets a golden color.
6. Serving: Toss the ravioli in the sage butter sauce, garnish with roasted pumpkin seeds, and serve.

The Story Behind the Dish
Pumpkin and Ricotta Stuffed Ravioli is a dish that brings the warmth and coziness of autumn to your table. The bright orange pumpkin, a symbol of harvest and abundance, pairs beautifully with the creamy ricotta, creating a filling that is both comforting and indulgent. This dish is a celebration of the season's bounty, encapsulating the essence of fall in every bite.

Tips and Tricks
- **Pumpkin Puree:** For the best flavor, use homemade pumpkin puree. It's simple to make and offers a richer taste than canned.
- **Dough Thickness:** Ensure the dough is rolled thin enough to see the filling, but not so thin that it breaks when cooked.
- **Sealing Ravioli:** Press the edges firmly to prevent the filling from leaking out during cooking.
- **Sage Butter Sauce:** Don't overheat the butter; the idea is to gently infuse it with sage flavor without burning it.

Ingredients:
- 300g tri-color rotini pasta (green, white, and red)
- 1 cup cherry tomatoes, halved
- 1 cucumber, diced
- 1 red bell pepper, diced
- 1/2 cup black olives, sliced
- 1/4 cup red onion, finely chopped

For the Dressing:
- 1/4 cup olive oil
- 2 tbsp balsamic vinegar
- 1 tsp dried Italian herbs
- Salt and pepper, to taste
Fresh basil leaves, for garnish

Instructions:

1. **Pasta Preparation:** Cook the rotini in boiling salted water according to package instructions until al dente. Rinse under cold water and drain.

2. **Combining Ingredients:** In a large bowl, combine the cooked pasta with cherry tomatoes, cucumber, red bell pepper, black olives, and red onion.

3. **Making the Dressing:** In a small bowl, whisk together olive oil, balsamic vinegar, Italian herbs, salt, and pepper.

4. **Dressing the Salad:** Pour the dressing over the pasta and vegetables, tossing well to coat.

5. **Garnishing:** Garnish with fresh basil leaves before serving.

PASTA FOR THE SENSES

The Story Behind the Dish
Tri-Color Rotini Salad is a celebration of colors and flavors, mirroring the vibrancy of a summer garden. The tri-color pasta not only adds a visual appeal but also brings a playful texture to the salad. This dish is a favorite at picnics and gatherings, symbolizing the joy of sharing and the beauty of simplicity.

Tips and Tricks
- **Pasta Choice:** Tri-color rotini not only adds color but also holds the dressing well in its spirals.
- **Freshness is Key:** Use fresh, crisp vegetables for the best texture and flavor.
- **Dressing:** Make the dressing ahead of time to allow the flavors to meld together.
- **Serving Suggestion:** This salad is best served chilled, making it a refreshing choice for warm days.

Zucchini Ribbon Pappardelle with Pesto

Ingredients:
- 2 large zucchini (1 green and 1 yellow)
For the Pesto:
- 2 cups fresh basil leaves
- 1/2 cup pine nuts
- 1/2 cup grated Parmesan cheese
- 3 cloves garlic
- 2/3 cup olive oil
- Salt and pepper, to taste
Extra pine nuts and Parmesan for garnish

Instructions:
1. Preparing Zucchini Ribbons: Use a vegetable peeler or mandoline to slice the zucchini into thin, long ribbons. Set aside.
2. Making Pesto: In a food processor, blend basil leaves, pine nuts, Parmesan, and garlic. Gradually add olive oil until a smooth paste forms. Season with salt and pepper.
3. Combining: In a large bowl, gently toss the zucchini ribbons with the pesto sauce, ensuring they are well coated.
4. Garnishing: Serve garnished with extra pine nuts and a sprinkle of Parmesan cheese.

The Story Behind the Dish
Zucchini Ribbon Pappardelle with Pesto is a playful twist on traditional pasta dishes. Using zucchini as the "pasta" makes this dish light, refreshing, and perfect for those seeking a healthier alternative. The green and yellow ribbons not only add visual appeal but also a delightful crunch that contrasts beautifully with the creamy pesto sauce.

Tips and Tricks
- **Zucchini Ribbon Thickness:** Make sure the ribbons are not too thin; they should have enough body to hold up to the pesto without wilting.
- **Fresh Pesto:** Homemade pesto is key to this dish. Its fresh, herby flavor elevates the simple zucchini.
- **Serving Temperature:** This dish can be served either chilled or at room temperature, making it versatile for any season.
- **Nut Variations:** Almonds or walnuts can be used instead of pine nuts for a different flavor profile.

Butterfly Pea Flower Fettuccine with Alfredo

Ingredients:
For the Pasta:
- 2 cups all-purpose flour
- 3 eggs
- 2 tsp butterfly pea flower powder
- Water, as needed

For the Alfredo Sauce:
- 1 cup heavy cream
- 1/2 cup unsalted butter
- 1 cup grated Parmesan cheese
- Salt and pepper, to taste

Fresh parsley and black pepper, for garnish

Instructions:

1. Making the Pasta: In a bowl, mix flour and butterfly pea flower powder. Create a well in the center, add eggs, and mix to form a dough. Add water if too dry. Knead until smooth, then let it rest for 30 minutes.

2. Rolling and Cutting: Roll the dough into thin sheets and cut into fettuccine strips.

3. Cooking the Pasta: Cook the pasta in boiling salted water until al dente. Drain and set aside.

4. Preparing the Alfredo Sauce: In a saucepan, melt the butter over medium heat. Add the cream and simmer for a few minutes. Stir in Parmesan until the sauce is creamy. Season with salt and pepper.

5. Combining: Toss the cooked fettuccine with the Alfredo sauce.

6. Serving: Garnish with fresh parsley and a sprinkle of black pepper.

The Story Behind the Dish

Butterfly Pea Flower Fettuccine with Alfredo is a culinary spectacle, combining traditional Italian cuisine with the exotic allure of butterfly pea flowers, native to Southeast Asia. The naturally blue hue of the pasta provides a stunning visual contrast to the creamy white Alfredo sauce, making this dish a conversation starter at any dinner table.

Tips and Tricks

- **Pasta Color:** For a deeper blue color, you can add more butterfly pea flower powder.
- **Sauce Consistency:** If the Alfredo sauce is too thick, add a bit of the pasta water to thin it.
- **Serving Temperature:** Serve the dish warm to fully enjoy the creamy texture of the sauce.
- **Flavor Pairing:** The mild flavor of the pasta allows the rich Alfredo sauce to shine. Add grilled chicken or seafood for extra protein.

1. Garlic and Olive Oil Spaghetti (Aglio e Olio): The aroma of sautéed garlic and olive oil is unmistakable.

2. Truffle and Mushroom Tagliatelle: Earthy truffles and mushrooms create a heady scent.

3. Basil Pesto Penne: The fresh, aromatic scent of basil pesto is delightful.

4. Cinnamon and Pumpkin Lasagna: A sweet and spicy twist with the warm scent of cinnamon.

5. Rosemary Chicken and Penne: The piney aroma of rosemary infuses the chicken and pasta.

6. Smoked Salmon Fettuccine: The smoky aroma of salmon adds a unique scent.

7. Roasted Red Pepper and Goat Cheese Linguine: A sweet and tangy aroma that tickles the nose.

8. Lemon and Asparagus Spaghetti: Zesty lemon and earthy asparagus offer a refreshing scent.

Garlic and Olive Oil Spaghetti
(Aglio e Olio)

49

Ingredients:
- 400g spaghetti
- 1/2 cup extra virgin olive oil
- 8 cloves of garlic, thinly sliced
- 1 tsp red chili flakes
- Salt, to taste
- Fresh parsley, chopped, for garnish
- Grated Parmesan cheese (optional)

Instructions:
1. Pasta Preparation: Cook the spaghetti in a large pot of salted boiling water until al dente. Reserve about 1 cup of the pasta water before draining.
2. Cooking the Garlic: In a large skillet, heat the olive oil over medium heat. Add the garlic slices and cook until they are golden and crisp. Be careful not to burn them.
3. Combining: Add the cooked spaghetti to the skillet with the garlic and olive oil. If the pasta seems dry, add some of the reserved pasta water.
4. Finishing Touches: Season with salt and red chili flakes. Toss everything to combine well.
5. Garnishing and Serving: Serve the pasta garnished with chopped parsley and, if desired, grated Parmesan cheese.

The Story Behind the Dish
Garlic and Olive Oil Spaghetti, or Aglio e Olio, is a testament to the Italian culinary philosophy of using few but high-quality ingredients. Originating from Naples, this dish is a staple in Italian cuisine, renowned for its straightforward preparation and robust flavors. It's the epitome of comfort food, often cooked in Italian homes as a late-night meal or a quick yet satisfying dinner.

Tips and Tricks
- **Quality of Ingredients:** With such a simple dish, the quality of the olive oil and garlic is paramount. Use the best you can find.
- **Garlic Cooking:** The key is to cook the garlic until it is just golden. Overcooked garlic can become bitter.
- **Pasta Water Magic:** Adding pasta water helps to emulsify the sauce and coat the spaghetti evenly.
- **Customization:** Feel free to add other ingredients like anchovies, capers, or a squeeze of lemon for a different twist.

Truffle and Mushroom Tagliatelle

Ingredients:
- 400g tagliatelle pasta
- 2 cups mixed mushrooms (such as shiitake, porcini, and button), sliced
- 1 black truffle (or truffle oil as an alternative)
- 2 cloves of garlic, minced
- 1/2 cup heavy cream
- 1/4 cup grated Parmesan cheese
- 2 tbsp unsalted butter
- Fresh parsley, for garnish

Instructions:
1. Cooking the Pasta: Cook the tagliatelle in a large pot of boiling salted water until al dente. Reserve some pasta water and drain the pasta.

2. Sautéing Mushrooms: In a large skillet, melt the butter and add the garlic. Sauté for a minute before adding the mushrooms. Cook until the mushrooms are tender and browned.

3. Adding Truffles: If using fresh truffle, shave some of it into the skillet. If using truffle oil, you will add it at the end.

4. Creating the Sauce: Add the heavy cream and Parmesan to the skillet. Stir to combine and simmer until the sauce thickens slightly. If the sauce is too thick, use the reserved pasta water to adjust the consistency.

5. Combining: Add the cooked tagliatelle to the sauce, tossing to coat. Season with salt and pepper.

6. Finishing Touches: Drizzle with truffle oil (if using) and garnish with shaved truffle slices and fresh parsley.

PASTA FOR THE SENSES

The Story Behind the Dish

Truffle and Mushroom Tagliatelle is a dish that speaks to the heart of gourmet cuisine. Truffles, cherished for their intense aroma and depth of flavor, elevate the humble mushroom to a new level of culinary excellence. This dish is often associated with luxury and special occasions, celebrated in regions of Italy where truffles are a prized local ingredient.

Tips and Tricks

- **Quality of Ingredients:** The quality of the truffles and mushrooms is crucial. Fresh, high-quality ingredients will significantly enhance the dish.
- **Handling Truffles:** If using fresh truffles, use them sparingly as their flavor is potent.
- **Mushroom Variety:** Use a mix of mushrooms for a more complex flavor profile.
- **Sauce Consistency:** The sauce should lightly coat the pasta without being too heavy or too runny.

Ingredients:
- 400g penne pasta

For the Pesto:
- 2 cups fresh basil leaves
- 1/2 cup pine nuts, toasted
- 1/2 cup grated Parmesan cheese
- 2 cloves garlic
- 2/3 cup extra virgin olive oil
- Salt and pepper, to taste

Extra pine nuts and Parmesan for garnish

Instructions:

1. **Pasta Preparation:** Cook the penne in boiling salted water until al dente. Drain and set aside.

2. **Making Pesto:** In a food processor, blend basil leaves, pine nuts, Parmesan, and garlic. Gradually add olive oil until a smooth sauce forms. Season with salt and pepper.

3. **Combining:** Toss the cooked penne with the freshly made pesto sauce. Ensure all the pasta is evenly coated.

4. **Garnishing:** Sprinkle with extra toasted pine nuts, more Parmesan, and a few fresh basil leaves.

The Story Behind the Dish

Basil Pesto Penne is a celebration of simple yet bold flavors, originating from the Genoa region of Italy. The key ingredient, basil, is a staple in Italian gardens and kitchens, known for its vibrant color and aromatic qualities. This dish is a testament to the Italian cooking philosophy where a few high-quality ingredients come together to create something truly extraordinary.

Tips and Tricks

- **Fresh Basil:** The fresher the basil, the more aromatic and vibrant your pesto will be.
- **Toasting Pine Nuts:** Lightly toast the pine nuts to bring out their nutty flavor.
- **Quality of Olive Oil:** Use a good quality extra virgin olive oil for a richer flavor.
- **Pesto Consistency:** If the pesto is too thick, add a little pasta water to thin it out and help coat the penne evenly.

Cinnamon and Pumpkin Lasagna

Ingredients:
- 9 lasagna noodles
- 1 can (15 oz) pumpkin puree
- 1/2 cup brown sugar
- 2 tsp ground cinnamon
- 1/2 tsp ground nutmeg
- 1/4 tsp ground cloves
- 3 cups béchamel sauce
- 1 cup grated mozzarella cheese
- 1/2 cup grated Parmesan cheese

Instructions:

1. Preparing the Noodles: Cook the lasagna noodles according to package instructions until al dente. Drain and lay them flat on a sheet to prevent sticking.

2. Making Pumpkin Filling: In a bowl, mix pumpkin puree, brown sugar, cinnamon, nutmeg, cloves.

3. Assembling the Lasagna: In a baking dish, spread a layer of béchamel sauce. Place a layer of noodles over it, followed by a layer of the pumpkin mixture. Repeat the layers, finishing with a layer of noodles topped with béchamel sauce.

4. Adding Cheese: Sprinkle mozzarella and Parmesan cheese on top.

5. Baking: Bake in a preheated oven at 375°F (190°C) for about 40 minutes or until the top is golden and bubbly.

6. Serving: Let the lasagna rest for a few minutes before serving. Sprinkle with a dash of cinnamon for garnish.

The Story Behind the Dish

Cinnamon and Pumpkin Lasagna is a delightful twist on the classic Italian dish, incorporating the quintessential flavors of fall. The idea is to blend the savory elements of lasagna with the sweet and spicy notes of pumpkin and cinnamon, creating a dish that's both comforting and unique. It's a celebration of the harvest season, bringing warmth and joy to any autumn table.

Tips and Tricks

- **Pumpkin Consistency:** Ensure the pumpkin mixture is not too runny to maintain distinct layers in the lasagna.
- **Béchamel Sauce:** A creamy béchamel sauce balances the sweetness of the pumpkin and adds richness.
- **Resting Time:** Allowing the lasagna to rest after baking helps it set, making it easier to cut and serve.
- **Pairing:** Serve with a light salad to balance the richness of the dish.

Ingredients:
- 400g penne pasta
- 2 chicken breasts, cut into bite-sized pieces
- 2 tbsp fresh rosemary, finely chopped
- 2 cloves of garlic, minced
- 1/2 cup chicken broth
- 1/4 cup white wine
- 2 tbsp olive oil
- Salt and pepper, to taste
- Grated Parmesan cheese, for garnish
- Additional rosemary sprigs, for garnish

Instructions:
1. **Pasta Preparation:** Cook the penne in a large pot of boiling salted water until al dente. Drain and set aside.
2. **Cooking the Chicken:** Season the chicken pieces with salt, pepper, and chopped rosemary. In a skillet, heat the olive oil over medium heat and cook the chicken until golden and cooked through.
3. **Creating the Sauce:** In the same skillet, add the minced garlic and cook for a minute. Pour in the chicken broth and white wine, scraping up any browned bits from the bottom of the skillet. Let it simmer until the sauce reduces slightly.
4. **Combining:** Add the cooked penne to the skillet with the chicken and sauce. Toss to combine and heat through.
5. **Garnishing and Serving:** Serve the pasta garnished with grated Parmesan cheese and additional rosemary sprigs.

The Story Behind the Dish

Rosemary Chicken and Penne is a dish that brings the flavors of the Mediterranean to your table. Rosemary, with its distinctive, aromatic fragrance, is a staple in Italian cooking, known for its ability to infuse dishes with a touch of the rustic outdoors. This dish is a celebration of simple ingredients coming together to create a hearty and satisfying meal, perfect for family dinners or casual gatherings.

Tips and Tricks

- **Fresh Rosemary:** Using fresh rosemary is key for the best flavor. Dried rosemary can be used in a pinch but won't have the same aromatic impact.
- **Quality of Chicken:** Opt for good quality chicken breasts for tenderness and flavor.
- **Wine Selection:** A dry white wine works best for the sauce, adding depth without overpowering the dish.
- **Sauce Consistency:** Let the sauce reduce to intensify the flavors and coat the pasta nicely.

Ingredients:
- 400g fettuccine pasta
- 200g smoked salmon, thinly sliced
- 1 cup heavy cream
- 2 tbsp capers
- 2 tbsp fresh dill, chopped
- 1 small onion, finely chopped
- 2 cloves garlic, minced
- 2 tbsp olive oil
- Salt and pepper, to taste
- Lemon wedges, for serving

Instructions:
1. Pasta Preparation: Cook the fettuccine in a large pot of boiling salted water until al dente. Drain and set aside.

2. Sautéing Onions and Garlic: In a skillet, heat olive oil over medium heat. Add the chopped onion and garlic, and sauté until translucent.

3. Creating the Sauce: Pour in the heavy cream and bring to a simmer. Add the capers and half of the chopped dill. Season with salt and pepper.

4. Adding the Salmon: Gently fold in the smoked salmon, being careful not to break it up too much.

5. Combining: Add the cooked fettuccine to the skillet, tossing it with the sauce and salmon.

6. Serving: Serve the pasta garnished with the remaining dill. Accompany with lemon wedges.

The Story Behind the Dish

Smoked Salmon Fettuccine is a fusion of Italian and Scandinavian flavors, where the smoky, rich taste of salmon meets the classic Italian pasta. This dish is often seen as a luxurious treat, combining the opulence of smoked salmon with the comforting familiarity of fettuccine. It's a testament to the versatility of pasta, able to blend seamlessly with a variety of global flavors.

Tips and Tricks

- **Quality of Salmon:** Opt for high-quality smoked salmon for the best flavor.
- **Timing of Salmon Addition:** Add the smoked salmon towards the end of cooking to maintain its delicate texture.
- **Cream Sauce Consistency:** The sauce should be creamy but not too thick, coating the pasta evenly.
- **Dill Pairing:** Fresh dill complements the salmon perfectly, adding a light, herby freshness to the dish.

Roasted Red Pepper and Goat Cheese Linguine

Ingredients:
- 400g linguine pasta
- 2 large red bell peppers
- 1 cup goat cheese, crumbled
- 2 cloves garlic, minced
- 1/2 cup olive oil
- 1/4 cup fresh basil, chopped
- 1/4 cup black olives, sliced
- Salt and pepper, to taste

Instructions:
1. Roasting the Peppers: Preheat your oven to 400°F (200°C). Place the red peppers on a baking sheet and roast until the skin is blistered and charred. Remove from the oven, cover with foil for 10 minutes, then peel and chop.

2. Pasta Preparation: Cook the linguine in boiling salted water until al dente. Drain and set aside.

3. Making the Sauce: In a blender, combine the roasted red peppers, garlic, and olive oil. Blend until smooth. Season with salt and pepper.

4. Combining: Toss the cooked linguine with the roasted red pepper sauce. Gently fold in the crumbled goat cheese.

5. Garnishing and Serving: Serve the pasta garnished with chopped basil and black olives.

The Story Behind the Dish
Roasted Red Pepper and Goat Cheese Linguine is a dish that celebrates the simple yet bold flavors of the Mediterranean. The sweet and smoky aroma of roasted red peppers pairs exquisitely with the tangy creaminess of goat cheese, creating a taste profile that's both comforting and sophisticated. This dish is a tribute to the art of balancing flavors and textures, turning everyday ingredients into a culinary masterpiece.

Tips and Tricks
- **Roasting Technique:** Roasting the peppers intensifies their natural sweetness and adds a smoky depth.
- **Quality of Goat Cheese:** Opt for a good quality goat cheese for a creamier texture and richer flavor.
- **Sauce Consistency:** Adjust the thickness of the sauce to your liking by adding more olive oil or some pasta water.
- **Basil for Freshness:** Fresh basil not only adds color but also a fresh, herby aroma that complements the other flavors.

Lemon and Asparagus Spaghetti

Ingredients:
- 400g spaghetti
- 1 bunch of asparagus, trimmed and cut into pieces
- Zest and juice of 2 lemons
- 1/4 cup olive oil
- 2 cloves garlic, minced
- 1/2 cup grated Parmesan cheese, plus more for garnish
- Salt and pepper, to taste
- Parmesan shavings, for garnish

Instructions:
1. **Pasta Preparation:** Cook the spaghetti in boiling salted water until al dente. Drain, reserving 1 cup of pasta water.
2. **Cooking Asparagus:** In a skillet, heat a little olive oil over medium heat. Add the asparagus and cook until tender but still crisp.
3. **Making Lemon Sauce:** In the same skillet, add the minced garlic and cook for a minute. Stir in the lemon zest and juice. Add the cooked spaghetti and toss to combine. If the pasta seems dry, add some reserved pasta water.
4. **Finishing Touches:** Stir in the grated Parmesan cheese and season with salt and pepper.
5. **Serving:** Serve the pasta garnished with Parmesan shavings.

The Story Behind the Dish

Lemon and Asparagus Spaghetti is a dish that sings with the freshness of spring. Asparagus, with its vibrant green and slightly grassy flavor, pairs wonderfully with the bright, acidic burst of lemon. This dish is a favorite in regions where asparagus grows abundantly, often heralding the arrival of warmer weather and the bounty of spring produce.

Tips and Tricks

- **Freshness of Asparagus:** Choose fresh, firm asparagus spears for the best flavor and texture.
- **Lemon Zest:** Use the zest as well as the juice of the lemon for a more intense citrus flavor.
- **Pasta Water Magic:** Adding pasta water helps to create a light sauce that clings to the spaghetti.
- **Cheese Choice:** Freshly grated Parmesan adds a salty, nutty depth to the dish.

1. Spicy Arrabbiata Penne: A bold and fiery taste that lingers on your palate.

2. Salty Pancetta and Pea Carbonara: A perfect balance of salty pancetta with sweet peas.

3. Sweet and Sour Sicilian Caponata Pasta: A delightful play of sweet eggplant and tangy vinegar.

4. Bitter Broccoli Rabe and Sausage Orecchiette: Bitter greens contrasted with savory sausage.

5. Sour Lemon and Herb Spaghetti: A tart and zesty flavor that awakens the taste buds.

6. Umami Mushroom Ravioli in Soy Butter Sauce: Rich in umami with a savory soy butter.

7. Savory Beef Bolognese with Pappardelle: A classic savory and meaty sauce.

8. Creamy Gorgonzola and Walnut Fettuccine: A rich, creamy taste with a nutty undertone.

Spicy Arrabbiata Penne

Ingredients:
- 400g penne pasta
- 1 can (400g) crushed tomatoes
- 3 cloves of garlic, minced
- 2 tsp red chili flakes (adjust to taste)
- 1/4 cup olive oil
- Salt and pepper, to taste
- Fresh basil leaves, for garnish
- Grated Parmesan cheese, for serving

Instructions:
1. **Pasta Preparation:** Cook the penne in a large pot of boiling salted water until al dente. Drain and set aside.
2. **Making the Arrabbiata Sauce:** In a skillet, heat the olive oil over medium heat. Add the minced garlic and chili flakes, sautéing until the garlic is golden. Stir in the crushed tomatoes, salt, and pepper. Simmer for about 10-15 minutes until the sauce thickens.
3. **Combining:** Add the cooked penne to the sauce, tossing to ensure the pasta is well coated.
4. **Serving:** Serve the pasta hot, garnished with fresh basil leaves and a sprinkle of grated Parmesan cheese.

The Story Behind the Dish
Spicy Arrabbiata Penne is a classic Italian dish, hailing from the Lazio region. "Arrabbiata" means "angry" in Italian, a nod to the heat packed in this dish. It's a favorite for those who love a little spice in their life. Traditionally, it's a simple dish, focusing on the quality of ingredients – ripe tomatoes, fragrant garlic, and fiery chili.

Tips and Tricks
- **Heat Level:** Adjust the amount of chili flakes to suit your spice preference.
- **Quality of Tomatoes:** Use high-quality canned tomatoes for a richer and more authentic flavor.
- **Garlic Flavor:** Don't burn the garlic; it should be golden and fragrant.
- **Freshness of Basil:** Add fresh basil at the end of cooking to maintain its vibrant color and aroma.

Salty Pancetta and Pea Carbonara Recipe

Ingredients:
- 400g spaghetti
- 150g pancetta, diced
- 1 cup green peas (fresh or frozen)
- 2 large eggs
- 1 cup grated Parmesan cheese
- 2 cloves of garlic, minced
- Black pepper, to taste
- Olive oil, for cooking

Instructions:
1. **Pasta Preparation:** Cook the spaghetti in a large pot of boiling salted water until al dente. Drain and reserve some pasta water.
2. **Cooking Pancetta:** In a skillet, heat a bit of olive oil and cook the pancetta until it's crispy. Add the minced garlic and sauté for another minute.
3. **Adding Peas:** Add the peas to the skillet and cook until they are just heated through.
4. **Making Carbonara Sauce:** In a bowl, whisk together the eggs and grated Parmesan cheese. Add black pepper to taste.
5. **Combining:** Remove the skillet from the heat. Add the drained spaghetti to the pancetta and peas. Pour the egg and cheese mixture over the pasta, tossing quickly to coat the pasta and cook the eggs with the residual heat.
6. **Serving:** Serve the carbonara immediately, garnished with extra Parmesan and black pepper.

The Story Behind the Dish

Salty Pancetta and Pea Carbonara is a twist on the classic Roman Carbonara. Traditionally made with guanciale and pecorino, this version introduces pancetta for its salty depth and green peas for a touch of sweetness and color. It's a dish that represents the creativity and adaptability of Italian cooking, turning simple ingredients into a symphony of flavors.

Tips and Tricks

- **Timing is Key:** Work quickly when combining the egg mixture with the pasta to avoid scrambling the eggs.
- **Quality of Pancetta:** Choose high-quality pancetta for a more authentic flavor.
- **Pea Selection:** Fresh peas are ideal, but frozen peas work well too. Just ensure they are thawed before cooking.
- **Creamy Texture:** The creaminess of carbonara comes from the eggs and cheese, not cream. The pasta should be coated but not swimming in sauce.

Sweet and Sour Sicilian Caponata Pasta

Ingredients:

- 400g pasta (like rigatoni or penne)
- 1 large eggplant, cubed
- 1 onion, chopped
- 2 cloves garlic, minced
- 1 can (400g) chopped tomatoes
- 2 tbsp capers
- 1/4 cup green olives, sliced
- 2 tbsp red wine vinegar
- 1 tsp sugar
- Olive oil, for frying
- Salt and pepper, to taste
- Fresh parsley, chopped, for garnish
- Pine nuts, toasted, for garnish

Instructions:

1. Eggplant Preparation: Salt the cubed eggplant and let it sit for about 20 minutes to draw out moisture. Rinse and pat dry.

2. Pasta Cooking: Cook the pasta in boiling salted water until al dente. Drain and set aside.

3. Sautéing Vegetables: In a large skillet, heat olive oil over medium heat. Sauté the onion and garlic until translucent. Add the eggplant and cook until golden and soft.

4. Creating Caponata Sauce: Stir in the chopped tomatoes, capers, and olives. Add red wine vinegar and sugar. Simmer for about 10 minutes until the sauce thickens. Season with salt and pepper.

5. Combining: Toss the cooked pasta with the caponata sauce.

6. Garnishing and Serving: Serve the pasta garnished with chopped parsley and toasted pine nuts.

The Story Behind the Dish

Sweet and Sour Sicilian Caponata Pasta is a celebration of Sicilian flavors, where the traditional caponata, a sweet and sour eggplant dish, is combined with pasta. This dish showcases the island's love for vibrant flavors and fresh ingredients, with the caponata being a staple in Sicilian households, often served as a side or appetizer.

Tips and Tricks

- **Balancing Flavors:** Adjust the sweetness and sourness to your taste by tweaking the sugar and vinegar amounts.
- **Eggplant Texture:** Ensure the eggplant is well-cooked to a soft, creamy texture.
- **Pasta Choice:** Short pasta shapes work best to hold the chunky sauce.
- **Serving Suggestion:** This dish can be served warm or at room temperature, making it versatile for different occasions.

Bitter Broccoli Rabe and Sausage Orecchiette

Ingredients:
- 400g orecchiette pasta
- 2 bunches of broccoli rabe, trimmed and chopped
- 400g Italian sausage, casing removed
- 3 cloves garlic, minced
- 1/2 tsp red pepper flakes (optional)
- 1/4 cup olive oil
- Salt and pepper, to taste
- Grated Parmesan cheese, for garnish

Instructions:
1. **Pasta Preparation:** Cook the orecchiette in boiling salted water until al dente. Drain and set aside.
2. **Cooking Broccoli Rabe:** In a large pot of boiling salted water, blanch the broccoli rabe for about 2 minutes. Drain and set aside.
3. **Browning Sausage:** In a large skillet, cook the sausage over medium heat until browned and crumbly. Remove the sausage and set aside.
4. **Sautéing Greens:** In the same skillet, add olive oil, garlic, and red pepper flakes. Sauté for a minute. Add the blanched broccoli rabe, salt, and pepper. Cook for about 3-4 minutes.
5. **Combining:** Add the cooked orecchiette and sausage to the skillet with the broccoli rabe. Toss everything together and heat through.
6. **Serving:** Serve the pasta hot, garnished with grated Parmesan cheese.

The Story Behind the Dish

Bitter Broccoli Rabe and Sausage Orecchiette is a classic Italian dish, beloved for its bold flavors. The bitterness of the broccoli rabe, a popular vegetable in Italian cuisine, is beautifully complemented by the savory richness of the sausage. This dish is a staple in many Italian-American households, often enjoyed as a comforting and hearty meal.

Tips and Tricks

- **Balancing Bitterness:** Blanching the broccoli rabe helps to reduce its bitterness.
- **Sausage Selection:** Use Italian sausage for authentic flavor; you can choose between spicy or sweet based on your preference.
- **Pasta Choice:** Orecchiette, meaning 'little ears' in Italian, is perfect for this dish as it holds the sauce and ingredients well.
- **Flavor Enhancements:** Add a splash of pasta water to the skillet if the mixture seems dry, as it helps to create a light sauce that coats the pasta evenly.

Sour Lemon and Herb Spaghetti

Ingredients:
- 400g spaghetti
- Zest and juice of 2 large lemons
- 1/4 cup extra virgin olive oil
- 2 cloves garlic, minced
- 1/4 cup fresh basil, chopped
- 1/4 cup fresh parsley, chopped
- Salt and pepper, to taste
- Grated Parmesan cheese, for garnish
- Lemon slices, for garnish

Instructions:
1. Pasta Preparation: Cook the spaghetti in a large pot of boiling salted water until al dente. Drain, reserving a cup of the pasta water.
2. Making Lemon Herb Sauce: In a large bowl, whisk together the lemon zest, lemon juice, olive oil, and minced garlic.
3. Combining: Add the cooked spaghetti to the lemon herb sauce. Toss to coat the pasta evenly. If the pasta is dry, add a bit of the reserved pasta water.
4. Adding Herbs: Stir in the chopped basil and parsley. Season with salt and pepper.
5. Serving: Serve the pasta garnished with grated Parmesan cheese and lemon slices.

The Story Behind the Dish

Sour Lemon and Herb Spaghetti is a dish that encapsulates the essence of Mediterranean cuisine. It's a tribute to simplicity and freshness, where the zesty lemon pairs perfectly with the aromatic herbs. This dish is often enjoyed in coastal regions, where the bright flavors mirror the sunny, seaside atmosphere.

Tips and Tricks

- **Freshness of Ingredients:** The key to this dish is the use of fresh lemons and herbs for a vibrant flavor.
- **Lemon Balance:** Adjust the amount of lemon juice and zest to your taste. The goal is a pleasant tartness without overpowering the pasta.
- **Herb Variations:** Feel free to experiment with different herbs like mint or dill for a different flavor profile.
- **Serving Suggestion:** This dish is best enjoyed fresh and can be served as a light main course or a refreshing side dish.

Umami Mushroom Ravioli in Soy Butter Sauce

Ingredients:
For the Ravioli:
- 200g all-purpose flour
- 2 eggs
- 300g mixed mushrooms (like shiitake, portobello, and button), finely chopped
- 2 cloves garlic, minced
- 1 tbsp olive oil
- Salt and pepper, to taste

For the Soy Butter Sauce:
- 1/4 cup soy sauce
- 100g unsalted butter
- 1 tsp sesame oil

For Garnish:
- Chopped chives
- Sesame seeds

Instructions:
1. **Making the Ravioli Dough:** Mix flour and eggs to form a dough. Knead until smooth, then let it rest for 30 minutes.
2. **Preparing the Filling:** In a skillet, heat olive oil over medium heat. Sauté garlic and mushrooms until tender. Season with salt and pepper. Let it cool.
3. **Assembling the Ravioli:** Roll out the dough thinly. Place small amounts of mushroom filling on the dough, cover with another layer of dough, and cut into ravioli shapes. Press the edges to seal.
4. **Cooking the Ravioli:** Cook the ravioli in boiling salted water until they float to the surface. Drain them gently.
5. **Making the Soy Butter Sauce:** In a pan, melt the butter, add soy sauce and sesame oil. Mix until well combined.
6. **Combining:** Toss the cooked ravioli in the soy butter sauce.

7. **Serving:** Serve the ravioli garnished with chopped chives and sesame seeds.

The Story Behind the Dish

Umami Mushroom Ravioli in Soy Butter Sauce is a fusion dish that marries the rich flavors of East Asian cuisine with classic Italian techniques. The umami-rich mushrooms provide a deep, earthy flavor that is perfectly complemented by the savory notes of the soy butter sauce. This dish is a testament to the versatility of pasta and its ability to blend with diverse culinary traditions.

Tips and Tricks

- **Mushroom Selection:** Use a variety of mushrooms for a more complex flavor.
- **Ravioli Thickness:** Ensure the ravioli dough is rolled thinly for the best texture.
- **Soy Butter Sauce:** Balance the soy sauce with butter to create a rich, velvety sauce that's not too salty.
- **Garnishing:** Chives and sesame seeds add a fresh and nutty finish to the dish.

Savory Beef Bolognese with Pappardelle

Ingredients:
- 400g pappardelle pasta
- 500g ground beef
- 1 onion, finely chopped
- 2 cloves of garlic, minced
- 1 carrot, finely chopped
- 1 celery stalk, finely chopped
- 1 can (400g) crushed tomatoes
- 1 cup beef broth
- 1/2 cup red wine
- 2 tbsp olive oil
- Grated Parmesan cheese, for serving

Instructions:
1. **Sautéing Vegetables and Beef:** In a large skillet, heat the olive oil over medium heat. Add the onion, garlic, carrot, and celery, sautéing until soft. Add the ground beef and cook until browned.
2. **Creating the Bolognese Sauce:** Pour in the red wine and let it simmer until reduced. Add the crushed tomatoes and beef broth. Season with salt and pepper. Simmer on low heat for about 1 hour until the sauce thickens.
3. **Cooking the Pappardelle:** In a separate pot, cook the pappardelle until al dente. Drain and set aside.
4. **Combining:** Toss the cooked pappardelle with the bolognese sauce, ensuring the pasta is well coated.
5. **Serving:** Serve the pasta hot, garnished with fresh basil and a generous sprinkle of Parmesan cheese.

The Story Behind the Dish

Savory Beef Bolognese with Pappardelle is a classic of Italian cuisine, originating from Bologna. The dish is a symbol of Italian culinary tradition, where slow cooking and rich flavors are celebrated. The wide ribbons of pappardelle are perfect for holding the hearty bolognese sauce, making each bite a perfect combination of pasta and sauce.

Tips and Tricks

- **Slow Cooking:** The key to a great bolognese sauce is slow cooking, which allows the flavors to develop fully.
- **Quality of Ingredients:** Use good quality beef and fresh vegetables for a richer taste.
- **Wine Choice:** A good red wine adds depth to the sauce. Choose one that you would enjoy drinking.
- **Pasta Water Magic:** If the sauce seems too thick, add a bit of pasta water to adjust the consistency.

Creamy Gorgonzola and Walnut Fettuccine

Ingredients:
- 400g fettuccine pasta
- 200g Gorgonzola cheese, crumbled
- 1 cup heavy cream
- 1/2 cup walnuts, crushed
- 2 cloves garlic, minced
- 2 tbsp butter
- Salt and pepper, to taste
- Fresh parsley, chopped, for garnish

Instructions:
1. Pasta Preparation: Cook the fettuccine in a large pot of boiling salted water until al dente. Drain and set aside.
2. Creating the Sauce: In a saucepan, melt the butter over medium heat. Add the minced garlic and sauté until fragrant. Pour in the heavy cream and bring to a gentle simmer.
3. Adding Gorgonzola: Add the crumbled Gorgonzola cheese to the cream. Stir until the cheese melts and the sauce is creamy. Season with salt and pepper.
4. Combining: Toss the cooked fettuccine with the Gorgonzola sauce, ensuring the pasta is evenly coated.
5. Adding Walnuts: Sprinkle the crushed walnuts over the pasta and toss lightly.
6. Serving: Serve the pasta hot, garnished with chopped parsley.

The Story Behind the Dish

Creamy Gorgonzola and Walnut Fettuccine is a dish that celebrates the harmonious blend of flavors and textures. Gorgonzola, with its distinctive blue veins and creamy texture, offers a deep and complex flavor that is beautifully balanced by the crunchy, nutty walnuts. This dish is a favorite in regions where Gorgonzola cheese is produced, reflecting the local ingredients and culinary traditions.

Tips and Tricks

- **Cheese Quality:** Use a good quality Gorgonzola for the best flavor.
- **Sauce Consistency:** Adjust the thickness of the sauce with more cream or pasta water as needed.
- **Walnut Crunch:** Toast the walnuts lightly for an enhanced flavor and crunch.
- **Garnishing:** Fresh parsley not only adds color but also a fresh taste that cuts through the richness of the sauce.

Touch (Texture)

1. Crunchy Walnut and Spinach Pesto Farfalle: A delightful contrast of crunchy walnuts and soft pasta.

2. Silky Avocado and Shrimp Linguine: Creamy avocado sauce with plump shrimp.

3. Chewy Orecchiette with Braised Beef: Al dente pasta with tender, slow-cooked beef.

4. Rustic Whole Wheat Penne with Roasted Vegetables: A hearty, grainy texture of whole wheat.

5. Smooth Mascarpone and Tomato Fettuccine: Silky mascarpone melding with the pasta.

6. Crispy Baked Mac and Cheese: Creamy inside with a crispy breadcrumb topping.

7. Slippery Egg Noodles with Sesame Sauce: Glossy noodles with a slick sesame glaze.

8. Fluffy Ricotta Gnocchi with Sage Brown Butter: Light, pillowy gnocchi in a velvety sauce.

Crunchy Walnut and Spinach Pesto Farfalle

Ingredients:
400g farfalle pasta
For the Pesto:
- 2 cups fresh spinach leaves
- 1/2 cup walnuts, plus extra for garnish
- 1/2 cup grated Parmesan cheese
- 2 cloves garlic
- 2/3 cup olive oil
- Salt and pepper, to taste
Fresh basil leaves, for garnish
Extra grated Parmesan cheese, for serving

Instructions:
1. Pasta Preparation: Cook the farfalle in boiling salted water until al dente. Drain and set aside.
2. Making Spinach Walnut Pesto: In a food processor, blend spinach leaves, 1/2 cup walnuts, Parmesan, and garlic. Gradually add olive oil until a smooth pesto forms. Season with salt and pepper.
3. Combining: Toss the cooked farfalle with the spinach walnut pesto. Ensure the pasta is well coated.
4. Garnishing: Sprinkle with extra chopped walnuts, grated Parmesan, and fresh basil leaves.

The Story Behind the Dish
Crunchy Walnut and Spinach Pesto Farfalle is a modern twist on traditional pesto pasta. While classic pesto is made with basil and pine nuts, this variation uses spinach and walnuts for a unique flavor and texture. The dish is a nod to the versatility of pesto, showing how it can be adapted with different ingredients to create new, exciting flavors.

Tips and Tricks
- **Freshness of Ingredients:** Use fresh spinach for the best flavor in the pesto.
- **Toasting Walnuts:** Lightly toast the walnuts for the pesto to enhance their flavor.
- **Pasta Water Magic:** Reserve some pasta water to loosen the pesto if it's too thick.
- **Serving Temperature:** This dish can be served warm or at room temperature, making it versatile for various occasions.

Silky Avocado and Shrimp Linguine

Ingredients:
- 400g linguine pasta
- 2 ripe avocados
- 200g shrimp, peeled and deveined
- 2 cloves garlic, minced
- Juice of 1 lime
- 1/4 cup olive oil
- Fresh cilantro, chopped
- Salt and pepper, to taste
- Lime wedges, for serving

Instructions:
1. **Pasta Preparation:** Cook the linguine in a large pot of boiling salted water until al dente. Drain and set aside.
2. **Making Avocado Sauce:** In a blender, combine the flesh of the avocados, lime juice, and olive oil. Blend until smooth and creamy. Season with salt and pepper.
3. **Cooking Shrimp:** In a skillet, heat a bit of olive oil over medium heat. Add the minced garlic and shrimp. Cook until the shrimp are pink and cooked through.
4. **Combining:** Toss the cooked linguine with the avocado sauce, ensuring the pasta is evenly coated.
5. **Adding Shrimp:** Add the cooked shrimp to the pasta and gently mix.
6. **Serving:** Serve the pasta garnished with chopped cilantro and lime wedges.

The Story Behind the Dish
Silky Avocado and Shrimp Linguine is a modern creation that marries the traditional Italian pasta with the contemporary love for avocado. It's a dish that reflects the evolving palate of the modern diner, seeking to combine familiar ingredients in innovative ways. The creaminess of avocado offers a unique alternative to traditional pasta sauces, while the shrimp add a luxurious touch.

Tips and Tricks
- **Ripe Avocados:** Ensure the avocados are ripe for a smooth, creamy sauce.
- **Shrimp Size:** Use large shrimp for a more satisfying bite.
- **Lime for Freshness:** The lime juice adds a zesty freshness that complements the richness of the avocado.
- **Serving Temperature:** This dish is best enjoyed immediately, as the avocado sauce may change color over time.

Chewy Orecchiette with Braised Beef

Ingredients:
- 400g orecchiette pasta
- 500g beef chuck, cut into chunks
- 1 onion, chopped
- 2 cloves of garlic, minced
- 1 carrot, chopped
- 1 celery stalk, chopped
- 1 can (400g) crushed tomatoes
- 2 cups beef broth
- 1/2 cup red wine
- 2 tbsp olive oil
- Grated Parmesan cheese, for serving

Instructions:
1. **Braising the Beef:** In a large pot, heat olive oil over medium heat. Brown the beef chunks on all sides. Remove the beef and set aside.
2. **Sautéing Vegetables:** In the same pot, add the onion, garlic, carrot, and celery. Cook until softened.
3. **Creating the Sauce:** Return the beef to the pot. Add the crushed tomatoes, beef broth, and red wine. Bring to a simmer, cover, and cook on low heat for about 2-3 hours until the beef is tender.
4. **Cooking the Pasta:** In a separate pot, cook the orecchiette until al dente. Drain and set aside.
5. **Combining:** Once the beef is tender, shred it in the sauce. Add the cooked orecchiette to the pot, tossing to combine with the beef sauce.
6. **Serving:** Serve the pasta hot, garnished with fresh herbs and a sprinkle of Parmesan cheese.

The Story Behind the Dish
Chewy Orecchiette with Braised Beef is a hearty and soulful dish, rooted in the rustic culinary traditions of Italy. It's a celebration of simple, high-quality ingredients and the art of slow cooking, where the beef is transformed into a tender, flavorful component that complements the chewy texture of the orecchiette.

Tips and Tricks
- **Quality of Beef:** Choose a cut of beef that is well-suited for slow cooking, like chuck or brisket.
- **Slow Cooking:** The longer the beef simmers, the more tender and flavorful it will become.
- **Pasta Choice:** Orecchiette, meaning 'little ears,' is ideal for this dish as its shape holds onto the rich sauce.
- **Wine Pairing:** A robust red wine, like a Chianti or Barolo, pairs beautifully with this dish.

Rustic Whole Wheat Penne with Roasted Vegetables

Ingredients:
- 400g whole wheat penne pasta
- 1 red bell pepper, sliced
- 1 zucchini, sliced
- 1 eggplant, cubed
- 1 cup cherry tomatoes
- 3 cloves garlic, minced
- Olive oil, for roasting and dressing
- Salt and pepper, to taste
- Fresh herbs (like basil or thyme), for garnish

Instructions:
1. **Roasting Vegetables:** Preheat the oven to 200°C (400°F). Toss the bell pepper, zucchini, eggplant, and cherry tomatoes with olive oil, garlic, salt, and pepper. Spread on a baking sheet and roast for 25-30 minutes until tender and slightly charred.
2. **Pasta Cooking:** Cook the whole wheat penne in a large pot of boiling salted water until al dente. Drain and set aside.
3. **Combining:** In a large bowl, mix the roasted vegetables with the cooked penne. Drizzle with olive oil and toss to combine.
4. **Serving:** Serve the pasta garnished with fresh herbs.

The Story Behind the Dish
Rustic Whole Wheat Penne with Roasted Vegetables is a celebration of simple, nourishing ingredients. The dish reflects a growing desire for healthier, more wholesome meals that don't compromise on flavor. Whole wheat pasta, with its rich, grainy texture, provides a nutritious base for the bright and flavorful roasted vegetables.

Tips and Tricks
- **Vegetable Variations:** Feel free to use any seasonal vegetables for roasting.
- **Roasting Time:** Ensure the vegetables are roasted until they're caramelized to bring out their natural sweetness.
- **Pasta Texture:** Whole wheat pasta has a firmer texture, so make sure it's cooked al dente for the best experience.
- **Herb Infusion:** Fresh herbs add a fragrant touch to the dish. Choose herbs that complement the vegetables' flavors.

Smooth Mascarpone and Tomato Fettuccine

Ingredients:
- 400g fettuccine pasta
- 1 cup mascarpone cheese
- 1 can (400g) crushed tomatoes
- 2 cloves garlic, minced
- 1/4 cup fresh basil, chopped
- 2 tbsp olive oil
- Salt and pepper, to taste
- Grated Parmesan cheese, for garnish

Instructions:
1. **Pasta Preparation:** Cook the fettuccine in a large pot of boiling salted water until al dente. Drain and set aside.
2. **Creating the Sauce:** In a skillet, heat the olive oil over medium heat. Add the minced garlic and sauté until fragrant. Stir in the crushed tomatoes, and simmer for about 10 minutes.
3. **Adding Mascarpone:** Lower the heat and stir in the mascarpone cheese until the sauce becomes creamy and smooth. Season with salt and pepper.
4. **Combining:** Add the cooked fettuccine to the sauce, tossing gently to coat the pasta evenly.
5. **Serving:** Serve the pasta hot, garnished with chopped basil and grated Parmesan cheese.

PASTA FOR THE SENSES

The Story Behind the Dish

Smooth Mascarpone and Tomato Fettuccine is a testament to the versatility of Italian cuisine, blending traditional tomato sauce with the creamy luxury of mascarpone. The dish represents a fusion of flavors, where the rich, velvety texture of the mascarpone beautifully complements the tanginess of the tomatoes, creating a harmonious and indulgent experience.

Tips and Tricks

- **Quality of Mascarpone:** Use high-quality mascarpone for a richer, creamier sauce.
- **Tomato Sauce Consistency:** Let the tomato sauce simmer to develop its flavors before adding the mascarpone.
- **Pasta Choice:** Fettuccine works well with creamy sauces due to its wide, flat shape.
- **Fresh Basil:** Fresh basil adds a burst of freshness and color to the dish.

Crispy Baked Mac and Cheese

Ingredients:
- 400g macaroni pasta
- 3 cups cheddar cheese, shredded
- 1 cup mozzarella cheese, shredded
- 2 cups whole milk
- 1/4 cup unsalted butter
- 1/4 cup all-purpose flour
- 1 cup breadcrumbs
- 1/2 tsp paprika
- Salt and pepper, to taste

Instructions:
1. **Pasta Preparation:** Cook the macaroni in boiling salted water until just al dente. Drain and set aside.
2. **Making Cheese Sauce:** In a saucepan, melt the butter over medium heat. Stir in the flour and cook for a minute. Gradually whisk in the milk until smooth. Bring to a simmer, then remove from heat. Stir in 2 cups of cheddar and the mozzarella until melted. Season with salt, pepper, and paprika.
3. **Combining:** Mix the cooked macaroni with the cheese sauce. Pour into a greased baking dish.
4. **Breadcrumb Topping:** Mix breadcrumbs with the remaining cheddar cheese. Sprinkle over the macaroni.
5. **Baking:** Bake in a preheated oven at 180°C (350°F) for 20-25 minutes or until the top is golden and crispy.
6. **Serving:** Let it cool slightly before serving.

PASTA FOR THE SENSES

The Story Behind the Dish
Crispy Baked Mac and Cheese is a classic American comfort food, beloved for its rich flavors and satisfying textures. The dish has its roots in home-style cooking, often prepared for family gatherings and cozy dinners. It's a simple yet indulgent meal that has been embraced and adapted in various ways across different cultures.

Tips and Tricks
- **Cheese Selection:** A mix of cheeses adds depth to the flavor. Sharp cheddar provides a tangy taste, while mozzarella offers creaminess.
- **Sauce Consistency:** Ensure the cheese sauce is smooth and creamy before combining with the pasta.
- **Baking Time:** Bake until the top layer is just the right amount of crispy, without overcooking the pasta.
- **Variations:** Feel free to add ingredients like cooked bacon, diced tomatoes, or green onions for an extra flavor twist.

Slippery Egg Noodles with Sesame Sauce

Ingredients:
- 400g egg noodles
- 3 tbsp sesame oil
- 2 tbsp soy sauce
- 1 tbsp rice vinegar
- 2 tsp sugar
- 1 tbsp peanut butter
- 2 cloves garlic, minced
- 1 tbsp grated ginger
- Toasted sesame seeds, for garnish
- Sliced green onions, for garnish

Instructions:
1. **Noodle Preparation:** Cook the egg noodles according to package instructions until al dente. Drain and rinse under cold water to stop the cooking process.
2. **Making Sesame Sauce:** In a bowl, whisk together sesame oil, soy sauce, rice vinegar, sugar, peanut butter, minced garlic, and grated ginger until smooth.
3. **Combining:** Toss the cooked noodles with the sesame sauce, ensuring they are evenly coated.
4. **Garnishing:** Sprinkle toasted sesame seeds and sliced green onions over the noodles.
5. **Serving:** Serve the noodles either at room temperature or chilled.

The Story Behind the Dish

Slippery Egg Noodles with Sesame Sauce is a dish inspired by the flavors of East Asian cuisine. It's a testament to the simplicity of combining basic ingredients to create a dish that's bursting with flavor. The glossy, slick texture of the noodles dressed in sesame sauce offers a delightful eating experience, making it a popular choice in both home cooking and street food markets.

Tips and Tricks

- **Noodle Texture:** Rinse the noodles in cold water after cooking to keep them from sticking together and to maintain a perfect texture.
- **Sauce Consistency:** Adjust the thickness of the sauce by adding a bit more sesame oil or water if needed.
- **Flavor Balance:** The combination of ingredients in the sauce should result in a balance of savory, sweet, and tangy.
- **Variations:** Add a protein like chicken, shrimp, or tofu to make it a more substantial meal.

Fluffy Ricotta Gnocchi with Sage Brown Butter

Ingredients:
For the Gnocchi:
- 500g ricotta cheese
- 1 egg
- 1/2 cup grated Parmesan cheese
- 1 1/2 cups all-purpose flour, plus more for dusting
- Salt and nutmeg, to taste
For the Sauce:
- 100g unsalted butter
- A handful of fresh sage leaves
- Salt and pepper, to taste
- Grated Parmesan cheese, for garnish

Instructions:
1. Making the Gnocchi: In a bowl, mix the ricotta, egg, Parmesan, a pinch of nutmeg, and salt. Gradually add flour until a soft dough forms. On a floured surface, roll the dough into long snakes, then cut into gnocchi-sized pieces.
2. Cooking the Gnocchi: Bring a pot of salted water to a boil. Cook the gnocchi in batches until they float to the top, then remove with a slotted spoon.
3. Preparing Sage Brown Butter: In a skillet, melt the butter over medium heat. Add the sage leaves and cook until the butter turns a golden-brown color. Season with salt and pepper.
4. Combining: Toss the cooked gnocchi in the sage brown butter sauce.
5. Serving: Serve the gnocchi hot, garnished with grated Parmesan and additional sage leaves.

The Story Behind the Dish

Fluffy Ricotta Gnocchi with Sage Brown Butter is a dish that brings together the rustic charm of Italian cuisine with the elegance of fine dining. Ricotta gnocchi, known for their lighter texture compared to potato gnocchi, offer a delicate and airy eating experience. The sage brown butter sauce, with its rich and aromatic flavor, perfectly complements the soft gnocchi.

Tips and Tricks

- **Ricotta Texture:** Drain the ricotta well to ensure the gnocchi dough isn't too wet.
- **Gnocchi Size:** Keep the gnocchi small and uniform for even cooking.
- **Browning the Butter:** Watch the butter closely as it browns to prevent burning.
- **Serving Suggestion:** This dish is best enjoyed immediately while the flavors and textures are at their peak.

1. Sizzling Bacon and Tomato Spaghetti: The crackle of bacon as it cooks with the pasta.

2. Crackling Spinach and Pine Nut Fusilli: The sound of pine nuts popping in the pan.

3. Popping Cherry Tomato and Basil Penne: The burst of tomatoes as they cook.

4. Crunching Crouton Caesar Pasta Salad: Croutons add an audible crunch to each bite.

5. Squishing Fresh Mozzarella and Tomato Caprese Pasta: The soft squish of fresh mozzarella.

6. Fizzing Lemon and White Wine Linguine: The fizz of white wine as it reduces.

7. Roaring Boiling Water for Classic Spaghetti: The foundational sound of pasta cooking.

8. Clattering Tossed Greek Pasta Salad: The clatter of olives and feta being tossed with pasta.

Sizzling Bacon and Tomato Spaghetti

Ingredients:
- 400g spaghetti
- 200g bacon, chopped
- 1 can (400g) chopped tomatoes
- 2 cloves garlic, minced
- 1 onion, chopped
- 2 tbsp olive oil
- Salt and pepper, to taste
- Grated Parmesan cheese, for garnish
- Fresh basil leaves, for garnish

Instructions:
1. **Cooking the Pasta:** Cook the spaghetti in a large pot of boiling salted water until al dente. Drain and set aside.
2. **Preparing the Bacon:** In a skillet, cook the chopped bacon over medium heat until crispy. Remove the bacon and set aside, leaving the bacon fat in the skillet.
3. **Making the Sauce:** In the same skillet, add the olive oil, onion, and garlic. Cook until the onion is translucent. Stir in the chopped tomatoes and simmer for about 10 minutes. Season with salt and pepper.
4. **Combining:** Add the cooked spaghetti and crispy bacon to the tomato sauce. Toss to combine and heat through.
5. **Serving:** Serve the pasta hot, garnished with grated Parmesan cheese and fresh basil leaves.

The Story Behind the Dish

Sizzling Bacon and Tomato Spaghetti is a dish that perfectly exemplifies the joy of simple, hearty cooking. The bacon adds a smoky, savory depth to the fresh tomato sauce, creating a harmonious blend of flavors. It's a dish that's often enjoyed in casual settings, embodying the warmth and comfort of home cooking.

Tips and Tricks

- **Bacon Crispiness:** Cook the bacon until it's just crispy enough to add texture to the dish.
- **Fresh Tomatoes Option:** You can use fresh tomatoes instead of canned for a fresher flavor.
- **Pasta Water:** Reserve some pasta water to adjust the sauce's consistency if needed.
- **Herb Freshness:** Adding fresh basil at the end retains its vibrant color and aroma.

Crackling Spinach and Pine Nut Fusilli

Ingredients:
- 400g fusilli pasta
- 2 cups fresh spinach leaves
- 1/2 cup pine nuts
- 3 cloves garlic, minced
- 1/4 cup olive oil
- Salt and pepper, to taste
- Grated Parmesan cheese, for garnish
- Chili flakes, for garnish (optional)

Instructions:
1. **Pasta Preparation:** Cook the fusilli in a large pot of boiling salted water until al dente. Drain and set aside.
2. **Toasting Pine Nuts:** In a dry skillet, toast the pine nuts over medium heat until they start to turn golden and release their aroma. Be careful not to burn them. Set aside.
3. **Sautéing Spinach:** In the same skillet, heat olive oil and sauté the minced garlic until fragrant. Add the spinach leaves and cook until just wilted.
4. **Combining:** Add the cooked fusilli to the skillet with the spinach. Toss in the toasted pine nuts. Season with salt and pepper.
5. **Serving:** Serve the pasta hot, garnished with grated Parmesan cheese and a sprinkle of chili flakes if desired.

The Story Behind the Dish

Crackling Spinach and Pine Nut Fusilli is a dish that celebrates the joy of simple, yet flavorful ingredients. The sound of pine nuts crackling in the pan adds a sensory delight to the cooking process, while the combination of nutty and leafy flavors creates a harmonious taste profile. This dish is often enjoyed in regions where pine nuts are a staple ingredient, reflecting the local culinary traditions.

Tips and Tricks

- **Pine Nut Watchfulness:** Keep an eye on the pine nuts as they toast, as they can burn quickly.
- **Fresh Spinach:** Use fresh spinach for the best flavor and texture.
- **Pasta Water Magic:** Reserve some pasta water to add to the dish if it seems dry, helping to create a light sauce that coats the pasta evenly.
- **Variations:** Feel free to add other vegetables or proteins to this dish for added nutrition and flavor.

Popping Cherry Tomato and Basil Penne

Ingredients:
- 400g penne pasta
- 2 cups cherry tomatoes
- 1 bunch fresh basil, torn
- 3 cloves garlic, minced
- 1/4 cup extra virgin olive oil
- Salt and pepper, to taste
- Grated Parmesan cheese, for garnish

Instructions:
1. **Pasta Preparation:** Cook the penne in a large pot of boiling salted water until al dente. Drain and set aside.
2. **Cooking Tomatoes:** In a skillet, heat the olive oil over medium heat. Add the garlic and sauté until fragrant. Add the cherry tomatoes and cook until they start to burst, releasing their juices.
3. **Combining:** Add the cooked penne to the skillet with the tomatoes. Toss with torn basil leaves. Season with salt and pepper.
4. **Serving:** Serve the pasta hot, garnished with grated Parmesan cheese.

The Story Behind the Dish

Popping Cherry Tomato and Basil Penne is a celebration of the garden's bounty, where the sweetness of ripe cherry tomatoes meets the aromatic freshness of basil. This dish is often enjoyed in the summer months when tomatoes are at their peak, offering a burst of flavor with every bite.

Tips and Tricks

- **Cherry Tomato Selection:** Choose ripe cherry tomatoes for the best flavor and juiciness.
- **Bursting the Tomatoes:** Cook the tomatoes just until they burst to release their flavorful juices.
- **Fresh Basil:** Add basil at the end of cooking to preserve its vibrant color and fresh flavor.
- **Pasta Choice:** Penne is ideal for this dish as it catches the tomato juices and bits of basil.

Crunching Crouton Caesar Pasta Salad

Ingredients:
- 400g pasta (like fusilli or rotini)
- 2 cups romaine lettuce, chopped
- 1 cup croutons
- 1/2 cup Caesar dressing
- 1/2 cup grated Parmesan cheese
- 2 cloves garlic, minced
- 1 lemon, for wedges
- Black pepper, to taste
- Olive oil, for cooking

Instructions:
1. **Pasta Preparation:** Cook the pasta in a large pot of boiling salted water until al dente. Drain and rinse under cold water to cool.
2. **Preparing Lettuce:** In a large salad bowl, toss the chopped romaine lettuce with a bit of olive oil and minced garlic.
3. **Assembling the Salad:** Add the cooled pasta to the bowl with the lettuce. Pour the Caesar dressing over the pasta and lettuce, and toss until well coated.
4. **Adding Croutons:** Just before serving, mix in the croutons to maintain their crunch.
5. **Finishing Touches:** Top the salad with grated Parmesan cheese and a sprinkle of black pepper. Serve with lemon wedges on the side.

The Story Behind the Dish
Crunching Crouton Caesar Pasta Salad is a playful twist on the classic Caesar salad, incorporating pasta to make it a more substantial meal. The addition of croutons not only adds a textural contrast but also introduces an auditory element to the eating experience, making each bite both flavorful and fun.

Tips and Tricks
- **Crouton Crunch:** Add the croutons just before serving to keep them crunchy.
- **Dressing Choice:** Use a quality Caesar dressing for the best flavor, or make your own for a fresher taste.
- **Pasta Type:** Short pasta shapes work best in this salad as they mix easily with the other ingredients.
- **Serving Suggestion:** This salad is perfect as a light lunch or as a side dish for a summer barbecue.

Squishing Fresh Mozzarella and Tomato Caprese Pasta

Ingredients:
- 400g pasta (like farfalle or penne)
- 2 cups cherry tomatoes, halved
- 1 cup fresh mozzarella balls
- 1/2 cup fresh basil leaves, torn
- 1/4 cup extra virgin olive oil
- 2 tbsp balsamic glaze
- Salt and pepper, to taste

Instructions:
1. **Pasta Preparation:** Cook the pasta in a large pot of boiling salted water until al dente. Drain and let it cool slightly.
2. **Assembling the Salad:** In a large bowl, combine the halved cherry tomatoes, fresh mozzarella balls, and torn basil leaves.
3. **Combining with Pasta:** Add the cooked pasta to the bowl with the tomato and mozzarella mixture.
4. **Dressing:** Drizzle the pasta and salad with extra virgin olive oil and balsamic glaze. Toss gently to coat everything evenly. Season with salt and pepper to taste.
5. **Serving:** Serve the pasta salad at room temperature or chilled.

The Story Behind the Dish
Squishing Fresh Mozzarella and Tomato Caprese Pasta is a delightful fusion of a traditional Italian Caprese salad and a hearty pasta dish. The soft, squishy texture of the fresh mozzarella provides a pleasant contrast to the al dente pasta and the juicy tomatoes. This dish is often enjoyed in the warmer months as a light yet satisfying meal, capturing the essence of Italian summer cuisine.

Tips and Tricks
- **Fresh Ingredients:** Use the freshest mozzarella and tomatoes you can find for the best flavor and texture.
- **Balsamic Glaze:** The glaze adds a sweet and tangy dimension to the dish, complementing the fresh ingredients.
- **Serving Temperature:** This dish is best enjoyed at room temperature to allow the flavors to meld together beautifully.
- **Variations:** Feel free to add additional ingredients like olives, cucumber, or grilled chicken for added flavor and texture.

Fizzing Lemon and White Wine Linguine

Ingredients:
- 400g linguine pasta
- 1 cup dry white wine
- Zest and juice of 2 lemons
- 2 cloves garlic, minced
- 1/4 cup olive oil
- 1/2 cup grated Parmesan cheese
- Fresh parsley, chopped, for garnish
- Salt and pepper, to taste

Instructions:
1. **Pasta Preparation:** Cook the linguine in a large pot of boiling salted water until al dente. Drain and set aside.
2. **Making the Sauce:** In a skillet, heat the olive oil over medium heat. Add the minced garlic and sauté until fragrant. Pour in the white wine and let it simmer until reduced by half, creating a light fizz.
3. **Adding Lemon:** Stir in the lemon zest and juice. Season with salt and pepper.
4. **Combining:** Add the cooked linguine to the skillet, tossing to coat with the lemon and white wine sauce.
5. **Serving:** Serve the pasta hot, garnished with grated Parmesan cheese and fresh parsley.

PASTA FOR THE SENSES

The Story Behind the Dish
Fizzing Lemon and White Wine Linguine is a dish that captures the essence of Mediterranean cuisine, where fresh ingredients and light flavors are celebrated. The combination of lemon and white wine creates a sauce that is both refreshing and slightly effervescent, offering a unique twist on traditional pasta dishes.

Tips and Tricks
- **White Wine Selection:** Choose a dry white wine that you enjoy drinking, as its flavor will be prominent in the sauce.
- **Sauce Consistency:** The reduction of the wine is key to concentrating the flavors and adding a slight fizziness to the dish.
- **Lemon Balance:** Adjust the amount of lemon juice and zest to your taste. The goal is a pleasant citrus flavor without overpowering the pasta.
- **Serving Suggestion:** This dish pairs beautifully with seafood, making it an excellent choice for a sophisticated yet easy-to-prepare meal.

Ingredients:
- 400g spaghetti
- 2 cups marinara sauce (homemade or store-bought)
- 2 cloves garlic, minced
- 1/4 cup olive oil
- Salt, for pasta water
- Grated Parmesan cheese, for garnish
- Fresh basil leaves, for garnish

Instructions:
1. **Boiling the Pasta:** Bring a large pot of salted water to a roaring boil. Add the spaghetti and cook according to package instructions until al dente.
2. **Heating the Sauce:** While the pasta cooks, heat the olive oil in a skillet over medium heat. Sauté the minced garlic until fragrant, then add the marinara sauce and warm through.
3. **Combining:** Drain the cooked spaghetti and add it to the skillet with the marinara sauce. Toss to coat the pasta evenly.
4. **Serving:** Plate the spaghetti, garnishing with grated Parmesan cheese and fresh basil leaves.

The Story Behind the Dish

Classic Spaghetti with Marinara Sauce is a staple in Italian cuisine, revered for its simplicity and comforting flavors. The dish represents the heart of Italian cooking, where quality ingredients and traditional methods come together to create something timeless and universally loved.

Tips and Tricks

- **Salted Water:** Generously salt the pasta water to give the spaghetti flavor from the start.
- **Sauce Choices:** Whether using a homemade marinara sauce or a quality store-bought one, the key is a rich, tomatoey flavor.
- **Al Dente Texture:** Cook the spaghetti until just al dente to maintain its texture and to absorb the sauce better.
- **Fresh Basil:** Adding fresh basil at the end adds a burst of freshness and color.

Clattering Tossed Greek Pasta Salad

Ingredients:
- 400g pasta (like rotini or farfalle)
- 1 cup Kalamata olives, pitted and halved
- 1 cup feta cheese, cubed
- 1 cup cherry tomatoes, halved
- 1 cucumber, diced
- 1/2 red onion, thinly sliced

For the Greek Dressing:
- 1/4 cup olive oil
- 2 tbsp red wine vinegar
- 1 tsp dried oregano
- 1 clove garlic, minced
- Salt and pepper, to taste

Fresh oregano, for garnish

Instructions:
1. **Pasta Cooking:** Cook the pasta in boiling salted water until al dente. Drain and rinse under cold water to cool.
2. **Preparing the Dressing:** In a small bowl, whisk together olive oil, red wine vinegar, dried oregano, minced garlic, salt, and pepper.
3. **Assembling the Salad:** In a large bowl, combine the cooled pasta with Kalamata olives, feta cheese, cherry tomatoes, cucumber, and red onion.
4. **Dressing the Salad:** Pour the Greek dressing over the pasta salad and toss to combine.
5. **Serving:** Garnish the salad with fresh oregano before serving.

The Story Behind the Dish
Greek Pasta Salad is a fusion of traditional Greek salad ingredients and pasta, offering a refreshing and filling meal. The dish is a celebration of Greek flavors, with the salty olives and feta, juicy tomatoes, and crisp cucumber, all brought together with a tangy dressing. It's a popular choice for picnics and potlucks, where its bright colors and clattering textures make it a delightful addition to any table.

Tips and Tricks
- **Pasta Choice:** Use pasta that can hold the dressing and mix well with the other ingredients.
- **Feta Cheese:** Add the feta cheese last to keep it from crumbling too much.
- **Chilling the Salad:** This salad can be served immediately or chilled for a few hours to let the flavors meld.
- **Variations:** Feel free to add other ingredients like bell peppers, artichokes, or grilled chicken for added variety.

Welcome to the glossary section of "Pasta for the Senses." This part of the cookbook is designed to help you understand some of the culinary terms used throughout the recipes. Familiarizing yourself with these terms will enhance your cooking experience.

Al Dente
- **Definition:** Italian for "to the tooth," used to describe pasta that is cooked to be firm to the bite. It should not be too soft or overcooked.

Braise
- **Definition:** A cooking method where food is first browned in fat, then cooked slowly in a covered pot with a small amount of liquid.

Deglaze
- **Definition:** The process of adding liquid (like wine, broth, or water) to a pan to loosen and dissolve the food particles that are stuck to the bottom after cooking or searing.

Emulsify
- **Definition:** The process of combining two ingredients together which normally don't mix easily, such as oil and vinegar. Often achieved by slowly adding one ingredient to another while whisking vigorously.

Julienne
- **Definition:** A culinary knife cut in which food items are cut into long thin strips, resembling matchsticks.

Mince

- **Definition:** To cut or chop food, especially herbs or garlic, into very fine pieces.

Reduction
- **Definition:** The process of simmering a liquid to evaporate its water content, which concentrates the flavor and thickens the consistency.

Sauté
- **Definition:** A cooking method that uses a small amount of oil or butter in a shallow pan over relatively high heat.

Simmer
- **Definition:** To cook liquid just below the boiling point (around 180-190°F or 82-88°C), characterized by small bubbles and gentle movement.

Zest
- **Definition:** The colored outer portion of the peel of citrus fruits. Used to add flavor to foods.

Understanding these terms will not only help you follow the recipes more easily but also equip you with knowledge that can be applied in various culinary adventures. Happy cooking!

"Pasta for the Senses" is enriched with special features that provide deeper insights into the culinary world, adding layers of interest and knowledge to your cooking experience.

1. Chef's Notes
- Personal insights and tips from the author on each recipe, offering suggestions for ingredient variations, plating ideas, and cooking techniques.

2. Recipe Variations
- For each recipe, alternative ingredients and methods are suggested to adapt the dish to different tastes, dietary requirements, or availability of ingredients.

3. Historical Anecdotes
- Fascinating stories behind certain dishes, tracing their origins, evolution, and cultural significance. For example, the history of Spaghetti Carbonara and its debated origins.

4. Cultural Insights
- Explore the culinary traditions of different regions, understanding how local ingredients, climate, and history have shaped various pasta dishes.

5. Pairing Suggestions
- Expert recommendations on pairing each pasta dish with the perfect wine, beverage, or side to enhance the dining experience.

6. Sensory Exploration

- Special focus on how each dish appeals to the senses, with suggestions on how to heighten each sensory aspect, be it through aroma, texture, or presentation.

7. Seasonal and Sustainable Cooking
- Tips on choosing seasonal ingredients for freshness and environmental sustainability, along with ideas for reducing food waste.

8. Interactive QR Codes
- Scannable QR codes leading to online resources such as video tutorials, additional recipes, or forums for culinary discussions.

9. Dietary Guides
- Detailed information on adapting recipes to fit various diets, including vegetarian, vegan, gluten-free, and low-carb options.

10. World of Pasta
- A section dedicated to exploring different types of pasta, from well-known varieties to obscure regional specialties, and how to best use them in cooking.

These special features are designed to enrich your cooking journey, making "Pasta for the Senses" not just a cookbook but a comprehensive guide to the world of pasta and culinary arts.

Sustainability in the kitchen is not just about what we eat, but how we prepare and think about our food. "Pasta for the Senses" encourages eco-friendly cooking practices, mindful ingredient sourcing, and reducing food waste. Here are some sustainability tips to consider:

1. Reducing Food Waste
- **Plan Your Meals:** Plan your meals for the week to avoid overbuying ingredients that may go unused.
- **Repurpose Leftovers:** Turn leftover pasta into a new meal, like a pasta frittata or salad.
- **Composting:** Compost vegetable trimmings and food scraps.

2. Sustainable Ingredient Sourcing
- **Local and Seasonal Produce:** Opt for locally grown, seasonal fruits and vegetables, reducing carbon footprint and supporting local farmers.
- **Ethical Protein Sources:** Choose sustainably sourced seafood and ethically raised meats.
- **Bulk Buying:** Purchase dry ingredients like pasta and spices in bulk to reduce packaging waste.

3. Eco-Friendly Cooking Practices
- **Energy Efficiency:** Use the right size pots for cooking and keep lids on to reduce energy usage.
- **Water Conservation:** Reuse pasta cooking water for watering plants or as the base for soups and stews.
- **Green Cleaning:** Use eco-friendly cleaning products and reusable cloths for cleaning up.

4. Mindful Eating
- **Portion Control:** Cook what you need to minimize leftovers.
- **Mindful Shopping:** Bring reusable bags and containers when shopping.

5. DIY Ingredients
- **Homemade Pasta:** Making pasta at home can be a rewarding way to reduce packaging.
- **Grow Your Own Herbs:** Cultivate a small herb garden for fresh, organic produce.

6. Community Involvement
- **Food Donations:** Share excess food with neighbors or donate to local food banks.
- **Educate and Share:** Encourage sustainable practices among friends and family.

Incorporating these sustainability tips into your cooking routine not only helps the planet but also enhances your relationship with food, making each meal more meaningful.

Conversion Tables

Cooking is a global language, and "Pasta for the Senses" embraces this by providing conversion tables to help both local and international audiences. These tables will assist you in accurately translating measurements from one system to another.

Volume Conversions
Standard US Metric (Approximate)
1 teaspoon 5 milliliters
1 tablespoon 15 milliliters
1 fluid ounce 30 milliliters
1 cup 240 milliliters
1 pint (2 cups) 470 milliliters
1 quart (4 cups) 950 milliliters
1 gallon (16 cups) 3.8 liters

Weight Conversions
Standard US Metric
1 ounce 28 grams
1 pound 454 grams
1/2 pound 227 grams

Temperature Conversions
Fahrenheit Celsius (Approximate)
32°F 0°C
212°F 100°C
250°F 120°C
275°F 135°C
300°F 150°C
325°F 160°C

350°F 175°C
375°F 190°C
400°F 200°C
425°F 220°C

Length Conversions
Standard US Metric
1 inch 2.54 centimeters

These conversion tables are intended to make the recipes in "Pasta for the Senses" accessible to a global audience, ensuring that everyone can enjoy the sensory delights of pasta cooking, regardless of where they are in the world.

Don't miss out!

Visit the website below and you can sign up to receive emails whenever S.R. Moore publishes a new book. There's no charge and no obligation.

https://books2read.com/r/B-A-XIBBB-RFNRC

BOOKS2READ

Connecting independent readers to independent writers.

Did you love *Pasta for the Senses*? Then you should read *The Secret of Lavender Lane*[1] by S.R. Moore!

[2]

Nestled in the heart of a quaint village lies "Emma's Eats," a charming bakery known for its delectable pastries and the warm smile of its owner, Emma Thompson. But the serene life of Lavender Lane is disrupted when a mysterious book falls into Emma's hands, unearthing a trail of long-buried secrets and a forgotten tale of love and loss.

In "The Secret of Lavender Lane," the tranquility of village life intertwines with the intrigue of historical mysteries. Emma, initially just a beloved baker, finds herself at the center of a puzzling enigma that dates back generations. Along with a cast of vivid characters including

---

1. https://books2read.com/u/bzrpkn

2. https://books2read.com/u/bzrpkn

the ever-punctual Mrs. Fletcher, the knowledgeable Tom Bennett, and the spirited Lucy, Emma delves into a web of hidden pasts and concealed ties.

As the story unfolds, the discovery of cryptic symbols and hidden messages in an old recipe book sets Emma and her friends on a quest that challenges the quiet history of Lavender Lane. From the cozy confines of the bakery to the vibrant community fair, the village's charming facades and Emma's world are cast in new light, revealing the layers of history and heart that pulse beneath.

Julian Spector, a once-celebrated but now forgotten author, becomes a pivotal figure in their journey, his own secrets woven into the village's history. The quest to uncover the truth not only reveals the depth of the village's legacy but also tests the bonds of community and friendship.

"The Secret of Lavender Lane" is a tale of discovery, a celebration of the simple joys of village life, and a testament to the enduring power of stories. It's a journey through the charming streets of Lavender Lane, where every corner holds a whisper of the past, waiting to be heard. Join Emma and her friends as they unravel the mysteries of their beloved village, where every discovery is a piece of a larger, heartwarming puzzle.